Nocturnes: Between Flesh and Stone

Poems by
Mary Kay Rummel

BLUE LIGHT PRESS ❖ 1ST WORLD PUBLISHING

1st WORLD
PUBLISHING

SAN FRANCISCO ❖ FAIRFIELD ❖ DELHI

Nocturnes: Between Flesh and Stone

BLUE LIGHT PRESS
www.bluelightpress.com
bluelightpress@aol.com

1ST WORLD PUBLISHING
PO Box 2211
Fairfield, IA 52556
www.1stworldpublishing.com

BOOK & COVER DESIGN
Melanie Gendron
melaniegendron999@gmail.com

COVER ART
Malibu Sunset by Charles Karp.

COVER CONCEPT
Mary Kay Rummel

INTERIOR ILLUSTRATIONS
Melanie Gendron

AUTHOR PHOTO
Steven Wewerka

FIRST EDITION

Library of Congress Control Number: 2020947175

ISBN: 9781421836775

Acknowledgments

Thank you to the editors who selected these poems, sometimes in different versions, for publication:

Still Life with Lemons, Oranges and a Rose, *Iris Literary Journal*, Assure Press and *Ekphrastic Review;*

After the Fires, *Martin Lake;*

A Medieval Herbal, *Water Stone Review;*

Conductor, *Fire and Rain: Ecopoetry of California*, Scarlet Tanager Press;

A Pandemic Story: Sister Theresa Louise, *Goodness*, Wising Up Press;

Desire and Stone, *Spillway;*

Fair, *St. Paul Almanac;*

From the Fires, *Borealis;*

Illuminator Dreams, *Nimrod;*

Latigo Canyon, *Psalms of Cinder & Silt*, Solo Novo;

Medieval Consolations, *Beer, Wine and Spirits*, World Enough Writers;

Music for a Sleepless Night, *Surprised by Joy*, Wising Up Press;

Night Birds, *Nimrod*; Heron poems by Minnesota writers, James Rogers, ed;

Nocturne, *Salt #2;*

The Spinning Universe: Konya Turkey, *Goodness*, Wising Up Press;

There Is a Bell Inside This Memory, *Spillway;*

Vanishing, *What Light*, Bright Hill Press.

Inheritance in an earlier version appeared in *This Body She's Entered* published by New Rivers Press

Thank You to Those Who Helped Make This Book Possible:

Diane Frank, Editor in Chief of Blue Light Press, who inspired and helped shape the poems. This book would not exist without her generosity and insight.

Charles Karp, for the cover painting, *Malibu Sunset;*

Melanie Gendron, designer for Blue Light Press;

Jean Colonomos, Lois Jones, Carl Phillips and Claudia Reder, for their blurbs;

Maia who has read many of these poems in various stages and whose insight into poetry is continually amazing;

Members of the Blue Light Press online workshop group who read much of this work in early stages;

Members of the Twin Cities writing group, Onionskin, Patricia Barone, Sharon Chmielarz, Carol Masters, Nancy Raeburn, Margaret Hasse, Ethna McKiernan, Kate Dayton and Donna Isaacs; Gwen Perun for her music; Sandra Rummel for her advice;

Members of California writing and community poetry groups: Marsha de la O, Phil Taggart, Florence Weinberger, Anita Puliers, Jean Colonomos, Ann Buxie, Elaine Alarcón-Totten, Marsha de la O, Gaby LeMay, Sharon Venezio, Nina Clements, Nancy-Jean Pément, Becky Sanvictores, Ron Alexander, Christine Kravatz, Lin Rolens, Sandra Hunter and Ken Jones;

Members of the Ventura poetry community who made me the first Poet Laureate of Ventura County;

The nonprofit Ventura County Poetry Project;

All the hosts who have invited me to read;

Editors who have published my poems;

Thanks always to my family — Conrad, Timothy, Miranda, Sylvie and Bridget, Ann, Andrew, Mari and Libby for their inspiration.

For Conrad,
Timothy, Miranda
Andrew, Ann

Table of Contents

1 After Basho 1

Illuminator Dreams 2
Nocturnes 4
Our Inheritance 6
Visitor 8
Hallowed Ground 10
A Turn Toward Red 12
Meditation on an Illumination 13
Roses and Monks 14
A Pandemic Story: Sister Theresa Louise 16
Still Life With Lemons 18
Jack Gilbert at VSC 19
The Songs 20
Music for a Sleepless Night 22
Among the Kingdoms 23
Finding Her 24

II Between 27

Finding Blue 28
Conductor 30
Alphabets 31
Vanishing 32
Great Blue 34
Latigo Canyon 35
After the Fires 36
Night Birds 37
Ways of Seeing 38
Haunted 40
Old Songs 42
A Swift History 43

III Where did our prayers go? 45

En Route 46
Derry in Time of Brexit 48
There is a bell inside this memory 50
Fair 52
Carving the River Caves 53
Beads 54
Crosby Dirt 56
Over Boneyards and Blossoms 58
Coming Home 60
Equinox 61
The Falling 62
Red, Wolf, Eclipsing 63

IV What's Left 65

Stone and Desire 66
In a Time of Distancing 67
Medieval Herbal 68
Blue Distance 70
Our Story 72
Medieval Consolations 74
From the Fires 75
Water Lilies 76
Red Fox Running 77
Ten Preludes in Blue 78
Starlight on Waves 80
The Colors of Pain 82
For All That is Lost 83
Blueing 84
The Spinning Universe 86
Illuminations 88
Notes 90
About the Author 91
About the Cover Artist 93

I

After Basho

Another year gone
Nun shoes on my feet
Poems in my hand

Illuminator Dreams:

An eleventh century nun in northern Germany,
scribe and painter

She copies the gospel
in a tower among oak branches.
She dreams of light
falling across the page.
shining through the leaves.
drawing her in and she writes
a story beneath the story.

Painting her dream light, she learns
underneath is more,
too much light to see
in the margins of the world.

With a hard tipped brush,
she dips into ultramarine
made from crushed lapis lazuli,
paints on calfskin, rests
with the tiny brush in her mouth,
wets it, readying herself
to paint Mary's blue gown.

Her painting like the scribble
of rain on the lake's wide page,
breaking off light, breaking off
when the light moves on.

She follows deeper, weary
inside the womb of rock, of rain.
She dreams of lapis stones carried
from Afghanistan by merchants
along that great silk road.
Stones worth more than gold.

Once she sat in sunlight
near a waterfall and once
she sang near the southern sea.

This is her story now,
and the light is hers forever.

In a thousand years, another woman will find
flecks of lapis in the nun's stone teeth
nested like tiny blue robin eggs.

Nocturnes

Joshua Bell plays his transcription
of Chopin, Nocturne #2 Opus 9

His violin carries me to Paris
where I walk alone in twilit shimmer
as street lamps, bridges shine with rain,
fog rising from the Seine.

The past is a stone in my hand.
I finger it as evening deepens,
plant myself on Pont de la Tournelle,
watch the back of Notre Dame as the sky
shifts through layers of blue.

Darkness shrouds the cathedral.
Even after the great fire,
the flat, dark skeletons of its buttresses fly,
softened by leafing plane trees.

I'm not alone here.
On the bank of the bridge
Sainte Geneviève lays her hands
on the shoulders of a child, a young Paris,
city she once protected from the Huns.

We're not strangers —
at eighteen I was given her name,
aching to become holy Sister Geneviève.

I, who never left St. Paul,
prayed to the protector of Paris
begging her to guide me
on sleepless convent nights.

She looks through sixteen centuries
down on me again,
no longer laboring to be holy.

Joshua Bell's violin distills blue
from Chopin's notes for piano,
the musk of centuries, gathering dusk.
A surge of strings against the night.
Past   present   future   one smooth stone.

Our Inheritance

All over Europe on last-judgment portals
of medieval cathedrals, Lust with his grinning belly
and ass's head, carries women to damnation,
nude women slung over his shoulder,
their hair hanging long.

On the left side of the main portal
of Chartres Cathedral, place of the lost, the damned,
one woman walks, is not carried, not nude, a nun,
all but her face veiled.

She smiles as she walks,
a message to generations of neck sore women.

As if she is saying,
It was worth it,
like nothing that ever happened before.

> *I love to look at you*, he said,
> *to talk while I am loving you.*

I closed my body for a long cold season.
In one brief transit I opened for him.

> *You smell so good to me*, he said.
> *I love to taste you.*

He loved my body.
With him my body was my soul.

> *I love to listen*
> *to your small sounds.*

I wanted to swallow him
in me, one heliacal rising.

On my knees in cold mornings,
I tried to exorcise him.
In the night when I beat my flesh
his face grew on my thighs.

In this city of God built by men
whom can I ask for forgiveness?

Why would I, who have broken out
of this book of glass written by men,
come back to the same death?

These circles that open into God
close down on a woman who knows
that body and soul are one.

Visitor

I still think of her
as a muse who would appear,
as a voice giving me direction.

Trying to find her I travel.
Ireland in the fog — is she there?

She hides behind birch leaves in a wash of light.
She's in the sheep looking for her lamb,
in the small thing, the way hummingbird
knows depths of the fireweed.

I climb through ruts,
track crisscrossing purposes.
The doe's lifted profile
at the field's edge, delicate as lace,
then her flight and the stillness after
as she listens and I listen

to white pines crossed by birches
their ghostly bare branches.
Each tree is its own road.
Even the foxglove travels,
even the bluebell.

I watch a turtle drag her heavy body
over the beach, think of her again
as I push my heavy body up
two hundred steps to Rocamadour,
steps made wavy from centuries of knees.
At the top the Black Madonna enfolds her child.

At Mary's House, hostel for pilgrims in Prague,
she stands in a silver scallop shell
dressed in a red and starry-blue gown.

She is everywhere.
If I glimpse her enough
will death be just another touch?

Hallowed Ground

1

The first time I flew alone to Paris,
I couldn't bring myself to step outside the airport
wrapping me safe in the over-familiar —
cash machines, zinc bars, scarf shops.

The Musee d'Orsay took away my fear,
brought me home to van Gogh's color madness —
to yellow fields behind St. Remy,
the circle-dance of indigo stars.

Walking along the Seine at night
as laughter drifted from green bateaus
and caught under bridges — loneliness
took me again to a breathless place
where I fell into a dimensionless blue,
one of Klein's models, covered in blue paint
lying flat, imprinted on canvas.

As I grow older, my pink-walled house is my refuge
like that Paris airport I couldn't bear to leave,
afraid of those who speak new languages,
stylish in black, scarves flung
in casual perfection around their necks.

2

I return to the church of San Clemente in Rome —
explore the layers of hallowed ground
below the upper church of glittering mosaics,
below faint murals of the early Christian level,

the lowest level, the temple of Mithras.
I wait with the Persian god of blood red waters.

The bell tower shakes with growling bronze,
bees wax candles, suggestions of shadows.

I hear in layered stone, accretion
of prayers, the pleading of centuries —

all that faith, all those beads, those bells
tolling my ebbing belief, eternal ocean
of human miseries, ocean of cicadas.

Here in the oldest place
where breathing starts and stops,
I remember Itzhak Perlman praying
on his violin, and I listen to all
the voices in that sea.

A Turn Toward Red

Cherries burn in their green nests
windows to a red world

Tiny finches steal them and so do we
a wilderness of bees in the garden

Flesh rose, guilder rose, hawthorn
and holly, the cardinal's racket

Red tide, the color of deep adobe
rolls relentlessly toward shore

Red weather in the heart

Unhindered red
a quick bright tongue lick

Unending flow of red
in blood we came

In blood we will go
a scaffold of stone

Crimson center of corona virus
being here is everything

Meditation on an Illumination

Woman Teaching by Giovanni Boccaccio

Holding the shimmering pages
before the scholars at her feet,
she teaches from illuminations,
binding these bearded tonsured monks
with lapis words, her hands of burnt air.

Gold, cherry, mineral,
monarch's wing call the eye to vellum
where the winds of spirits become visible.
Colors lighting from behind
a scrim, a veil over her fading years.

The language of butterflies,
pigments from the warm body
of the earth, cinnabar, ochre,
phosphor, gold swarming into air.

She points to the icons of a world
passing into a world to come,
and sends their starving souls soaring
on the planet's wings.

Roses and Monks: Birmingham, England

Though sometimes as we walk this earth, with the memories of
our loved ones shadowing us, we might also become our own holy
places: roaming churches, cathedrals and memory mausoleums.
                                    — *Edwidge Dandicat*

Before sunset, I walk muddy streets,
searching for morning light I missed,
find it in wet flesh of other peoples' roses.

The Pakistani woman at the corner grocery
confides, *I've lived here twenty-give years.*
As soon as my children are settled, I'm leaving
even if my husband stays.
I help her wrap roses — scarlet, coral and yellow —
her own bright colors and she adds,
I miss my mother and sisters.

I ride the train to Shrewsbury,
looking for the monks chanting
on BBC, wanting god-praise
in a cloister trembling with cold.

I find only one large rain-worn stone,
in Cadfael's restored medieval garden
of scurvy grass, hyssop, St. Mary's thistle
citron, cockscomb, apothecary rose.

Going back I dream the land beside the tracks
is lined with those who've lived before me.
My journey marked by grimy industry,
small back gardens waving laundry,
and graveyards, centuries thrown together —
black stones leaning in chaotic earth.

How can we travel this world without
the dead? We make houses for them,
offer roses, granite.

A Pandemic Story: Sister Theresa Louise

It was 1917.
Just fifteen, you kissed your mother and sister,
climbed the street car to Randolph Street,
walked a path through the woods
carrying your small travel bag.

Near the river, at the stone convent
framed by trees,
you entered through the heavy door.

On the feast of St. Joseph,
you rose in the dark, a poem
composing itself in your heart —

In the early morning light
I will dress myself in white
To give myself to you
Who gave yourself for me.

You knelt at the altar,
with just-shorn hair, in wool habit
and veil, repeating your new name,
Theresa Louise, Theresa Louise,
getting to know the sound and feel.

You slept, hungry,
with other young novices,
in white night gowns,
lithe as birches in wind,
hidden from each other
by white curtains
in a forty bed dorm.

Days in silence. After prayers, you
scrubbed stairs, watched your sisters
climb, some growing weaker.

On calloused knees you scoured
bathroom floors, then prayed some more,
studied Mary and Joseph
in stained glass above the altar

Theresa Louise, young heart
storing-up light, your voice chanting…

When your sisters fell sick in 1918
and your superior refused them medications,
saying *God wants us to suffer,*
did you still believe?

The dorm became an infirmary,
healthy sisters caring for the sick,
until a storm of flu killed all of you.

You were my father's favorite cousin —
your death, he said, was the greatest grief
in his twelve-year-old life.

Is being dead the end of your story
the book closed?
Is this poem the end of your tale?
I hold on to your prayers
even as they slip away.

Still Life with Lemons, Oranges and a Rose

Francisco de Zurbaran, 1633

Three ripe lemons reflected
in a plate of polished pewter —
breast shaped ovals in morning light,
shadows defined
by slanted autumn sun on stones.

Ancient motifs — the trinity, homages to the virgin —
oranges with blossoms, water in pewter for purity,
the thornless rose, shades of white and tissue pink,
immaculate conception to renaissance viewers.

It's the intensity of color that draws me,
that curls my fists and fingers,
lemony oil, pocked yet smooth skin.
My mouth tightening at the taste.

Round bellied oranges wear deeper shadows,
as do sinners who bite into fruit.

The background, obsidian
color beyond all colors, living pigment
created at the back of the brain,
bright as the history of shadows.
Each color a kaleidoscope
muted with gothic dark.

Jack Gilbert at Vermont Studio Center

Quote is from *We are the junction*

This poet is frail, shaking as he climbs
wooden steps to the stage
singer of the spirit body...

> *The mind touches the heart and is music.*
> *When body touches heart*
> *they, together, are the moon*
> *in the silently falling snow...*

Opening chasms of longing and desire
water on stone
shining with inner light as he speaks.

Once a perfect New England church, it seems
made for his shaman presence,
a bell for the light.

In the hush after he falls silent
I want to run, to merge
with mud and rush of the river.

The Songs

For John Berryman

We passed one day on the steps of Lind Hall
you late for class, wild hair, glasses askew.
I was just out of the convent, new in graduate school,
books bouncing on my back as I ran
down Church Street to join the marchers.

Five thousand strong on Washington Avenue they sang,
"We Shall Overcome," and then began the chant
that frightened me —
Ho Ho Ho Chi Min
Ho Chi Min is gonna win —
I couldn't sing — those jungles
hid my youngest brother.

At home I opened your *Dream Songs,*
blown away by your impertinent piety,
iambic the only verse I knew
until you brought to my ear
a new scripture —

> *A Buddhist, doused in the street, serenely burned.*
> *The Secretary of State for War,*
> *Winking it over, screwed a redhaired whore.*
> *Monsignor Capovilla mourned. What a week.*

You needled, wheedled me
not with beauty, but scarifying singe
created in all-night drunks, bruised
raging blues — your book of revelations.

I wanted some of that wildness in me.
As your songs freed my lines, my fears
your music moved in me,
how could I resist?
I was learning poetry and sex.

Three years later your body hit the rocks
below the river bridge I walked across.
My brother in the hospital,
my country was still bombing
Vietnam to kingdom come.

Music for a Sleepless Night

Lisbon — in the Alfama

Before she ever moans
from that world edge throat —
rough velvet, cigarette smoke and wine,
the diners begin to clap.

Her bare feet gripping flagstone,
a big woman, neither young nor old, that voice
tangled in long hair, baptized in dark water.
Dark sounds curl up from her feet,
from below ancient roots.

Something about her childhood, a broken heart.
Portuguese so close to Spanish
a word now and then floats clear.
Her *fados* always sung along this river
erupting from the silence of fish.

Her voice born where river meets sea.
She enters you at night,
with her liquid soul possesses you.

Among the Kingdoms

Sur le Pont d'Avignon — a nursery song

Your *Lonely Planet* has brought you to this —
impassable stone bridge, three quarters destroyed
by the king in the siege of twelve-twenty-six.

The villagers built a new bridge above the old one,
the way you build fresh dreams from scrap,
bright snatches of memory.

This palace once filled with men in scarlet robes.
Now black and white paintings of women, nudes
seem to be leaping with carnal exuberance
off the historic whitewashed walls
of the great hall of the pope.

The cooing of pigeons shivering on the altar
echoes among gold sovereigns once strewn
by guilt across the chapel floor, while sunset
scatters crimson coins on the Rhone below.

You have tears in your eyes
as you hum the nursery song,
the lilting way your mother sang it to you.
You always stopped crying and listened.

Finding Her: Mother Goddess on her Throne 5750 B.C.

Statuette in the museum of Anatolian civilizations from Catalhoyuk (a Neolithic town)

No more than terra cotta
warmed earth smell —
her thick body on a little clay throne.
Breasts like large loaves,
buttocks like melons,
flanked on each side
by lion-animals,
her hands, their heads
a melding of woman and beast.

Her taut belly protrudes —
a child's head emerges from between her thighs —
Paleolithic mother goddess, thunder heart
of the earth, of us all.

Before Aphrodite, older than Artemis,
her face lifts as she listens to her own music.
Hair piled on her head,
small nose, enduring mouth.

She is for walking
through sage, heat, locusts, war.
Her gravity reminds me
of my great grandmother Josephine —
in an old portrait, black Irish hair coiled,
wine-dark eyes,
body shaped like a hive.

Both found whole, surrounded
by ancient fragments of a puzzle,
humming an ancient note —
Listen, they say,
do you want to hear
all the women resting inside us —
in dirt, rock, chant, darkness?

I have traveled so far
to find her memory.

II

Between

I watch a young egret cross
blue stones with impossible feet,
ask music to dance
my syllables' small toes.

Finding Blue

I look for blue.
—Vincent Van Gogh

I am trying to live each day
as if it were the first,
an Eve waking and naming —
sun a surprise, wing a flash.

Along the pond just-emerged indigo
dragonflies loop and whir,
mad with sex and the ending
of their two week adult lives.

I read that early humans did not name blue.
Did they see it? What did Eve call sky?

I like to think two thousand years ago
a woman swerved off her path to kneel
before a blossom, its color a flutter of sky
she suddenly named blue, laughing,
bringing others to see.

Now ultramarine and indigo everywhere.
Feathers of hunting jays, the blue fire
of the Côte d'Azure in summer.

Braid in feathers of four wild turkeys
on the roof edge, the youngest afraid to fly.

Flight lessons for young mallards
almost but not quite lifting off, cobalt
flashing from their tails.

Cattails spear an electric sky
where heron drops to the green
swaddle of the pond.

Blue as storm, iridescent, alive
to the rings on the surface
where the turtle rises.

Dragonfly blue rushes through
a quick and private joy.

Conductor

In California, in the cold
a bundled child might think
she is a goddess of color.
She might conduct an orchestra
above saffron hills,
holding her baton of lupine sky
over bee fuchsia, setting in motion
the deep hum of creation.

Her arms become waves,
conducting purple shellfish,
beaded ribs, spoon-shaped nails,
sway of sea and dune grasses,
hair and sand.

She orchestrates
on patio, veranda, balustrade
where palm trees wear full-length scarves,
concealing the nests of rodents,
trailing perfumes of fennel and sage.

No wind, no rain.
Only slow white fog brushing piers,
Gregorian notes, rising, falling.

Blue cornucopias of wisteria
pour over balconies.
Bougainvillea guards the stairways.
Rosettes, umbels, sepals play old songs.
Cracked with clay, crusted with brine,
their scattered notes fly over the earth.

Alphabets

To play a wrong note is insignificant.
To play without passion is inexcusable.
—Beethoven

Write the way wind writes clouds
across the wake of swallows.

Write air as plants compose
stalks, leaves, a flower's plumed circle.

Write the heavy alphabet
of waves, fragile threads of foam.

Write the way water scribbles
tidelines, seaweed, shells, the thousand
feet of starfish, the song of mussels.

Write a surging spring,
cursive script of anemone,
beech and violet.

Write thunder over domed trees,
white gold of the strike,
lightning and wheat.

Write as autumn wind bends
the curvature of space.

Write winter like the beating heart
writes bone, scale, claw, tooth —
every whispering line.

Let ink flow over eyelids,
as fingers follow the infinite curve —
throat, hip, thigh — orbiting star.

Vanishing

We live by the mercy of things
no longer with us —
redwings in their swale of reeds.
the waterfall grown small,
creeping its way up the rock face.
Rain brushed wild roses
hidden in bogs,
pollen buried for eternity.

Wheat in the haze and heat
on its way down the rootstalk.
The ponderous winds
move slowly and sullenly,
the stuff of dreams
while the earth crackles
like peeling canvas
and everything
a human being is made of
sifts in the air.

Dove-blue plums
blown to feather particles.
Grey-white bindweed
crumbles beneath clay
where monarch, starling and lark
are lost for all time.

What will we be when the glaciers are gone?
Flood, echo and fire.
Let us see with an open, wide grief.

The disappeared,
where they were born and died,
shining all around us, the way
burned-out starlight glows
for a time
in the eyes of the living.

Great Blue

After Linda Gregg

If we don't see her standing
       in duck weed water,
if ripples do not wash her legs,
if lake air never becomes her shawl,
       there is no summer.
If she does not spread her wings,
       the cold will return.

She never brings winter, but if green
comes without her, where's the joy in it?

Before light, we make our way
through humming fields, calling her,
begging her to return — listening

for the whisper that wind makes
       beneath her wings.

Latigo Canyon

These mountains — electric yellow, wild mustard
glittering, a thousand crowns of sunlight.
This valley of poppies threaded
with lupine, fire and smoke.

I drive through remembering dust around a door frame,
smoke and voices pressing against that door.
A strong smell of winter, hiding, stories with edges
glowing, lightning glissade before the page burns black,
that line where fire lives and dies and lives again.

Blown up in smoke they say, a minute's burn,
racing toward and away,
that peeling a flower does, until it's not.

A living thing they call fire,
breath or no breath, the center which is not
the center but a door, and what leaps through.
Fire's odor and fire's roar,
the updraft and the cinders that will rain down
over what is spared and what is chosen.

After the Fires

When you close your eyes in such a silence,
death could come up behind you like an old friend
on tiptoe and touch you.
I'm afraid to breathe the air grown thick
with sinking smoke where sea is flat as glass.

No sound at first, nothing, and then,
as if out of the egg of silence,
small hatchings — thin fluting of a red finch,
the song sparrow's single note of warning,
a small egret's hoarse *broagh*.

In the distance a hawk's cry breaks off,
one twig crackles, slips free of another.
The tide's faint rustling — no end to its run,
a dry whisper, as ash in sand is shifting.

Night Birds

A night heron, head inclined, freezes, eyes intent.

Nothing gentle in this night bird who brings silence
to the pond, stops the laughing red-wing blackbirds
feeding among stones, ends jay's ululations — silence
from distant shores worn in her deep shimmer.

She turns away from me in her white gown and veil.
Old nun, round shouldered at prayer, she lifts her wings,
stares into tree visions, disappears in blue reflection.

All my life I've known these old women praying.
Now I'm one of them. Crone dreams I never wanted
live in the hollow oak outside my door.

I hear their shadow-voices, collect their spells
and verses, trade one night with its cloak
of threaded silver for another.

Ways of Seeing

Chiang Rai, Thailand
I'm just an absent minded tourist but I love the light.
                                    —*Adam Zagajewski*

I wander among the blooms of this small city,
savoring the slant of sunlight.

Beneath hibiscus, birds of paradise,
a snake and toad wrestle —
a white snake, thin, with a bronze stripe

along its forehead. Hinged jaws
spring wide as a hand, clamp
the toad's skull, squeeze

furiously as the captive thrashes,
hind feet scuttling,
a sumo wrestler twisting

in the grip of implacable appetite.
Snake-jaw still too narrow for the prey's girth,
such a slow dance after the quick strike —

toad-throat bulges, then disappears
the broad torso sucked down
that muscled gullet.

Bicycling villagers pedal over the bridge
spanning the slow dark
drift of the Mae Kok.

Snake raises its gaze above the grass,
waves the captive legs —
brown flag to a wilderness of bees.

Riders face straight ahead,
missing the struggle.

Yellow and green long boats
with red roofs and car engines
travel the river.

At two hours the last foot vanishes,
the snake's eyes blink.

In the river shallows, straw-hatted women
collect plump snails from the bottom,
drop them in a bag.

A gift today, simply to love the light,
to witness that snake's impossible feat,
to remember my own implacable hungers.

Haunted

They're back: Millions of cicadas expected to emerge this year
—NPR

The wind screams
I have news for you:

nests fall
cattails break
their shape is lost
cold seizes the bird wing
inside the earth
the cicada waits

•••

Don't clap yet.
It's a caesura.

•••

A migration of cicada
have left their shells
like mummy cases on the trees.

Unburied, hear them throbbing
beneath the ruins

cicada
cicada
cicada...
then thunder.

•••

Sting of surround sound —
its noise scrapes high
across the dry night air —
dull blades needing repair.

•••

It has nothing to do with age.
It's being willing to live in a beat
defined by its own tattoo.

Take your unsweatered body
outside. Do a wild dance.

•••

Metronome of summers
aural abacus of days
a sliver of time in the sun,
they shimmer then disappear.

If it's true, as the Irish say,
that cicadas are the souls
of dead poets crying out
the things they did not write
when they lived
I will pray to them —

Give me your voices, oh cicadas,
before your songs grow thin
in the dry weeds
along the railroad tracks.

•••

Nothing but isolation time, a waiting
as light breaks from the rotting cells of leaves
into the patient time of the cicada.

Old Songs

White bear rolls from his cloud
above the white pines.
Loon grieves the lake, her quaking
wail — a throat-cut soprano.

This bonfire at water's edge,
flames haunt every angle,
my soul hurries back like my mother
to wake me from a nap, singing
Lazy Mary, will you get up?

The moonlight croons from clouds,
delves darkness, loosens beams
that dream the pines
and ghost the birch trees.

Moon knows herself in her sounding
as the lake croons back.
I always sang in answer,
No, my mother, I won't get up.

Inside the cabin, a path worn in carpet
takes me to the window, to what lives
out there in the feral woods.

I keep thinking that if I go alone
into the seize of that silence,
I will know what to listen for,

root-filled airways, humming paths
ocarina moon, full of her own music.

Where I'm from is far —
but I am getting closer.

A Swift History of the River

The birds haunt me
full of wind-struck bluster,
full of sun-seamed visions,
quicksilver coins
over my current.

I'm not ready to stop singing.
Remember me slowly,
the way the Mississippi laves the shore
in the blue susurrus of summer.

Sand hill crane, one outstretched leg
invisible in the miracle of light,
remembers mud and returning
in high wind, rain torrent.

The blowsy river opens wide
her body for song.

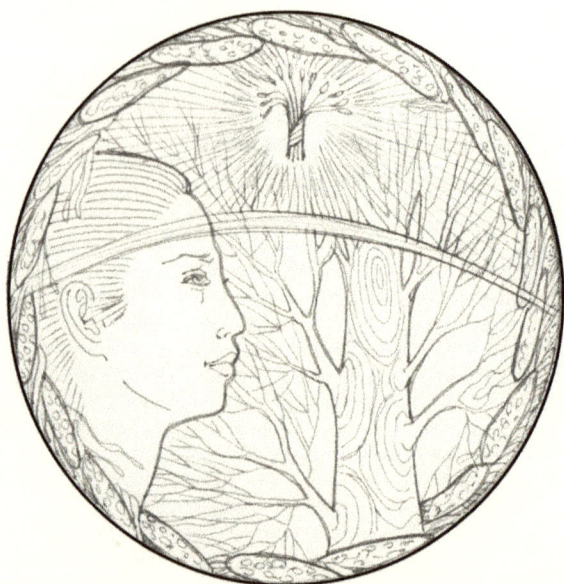

III

Where did our prayers go?

River of leaf-light
Tree of darkness who will embrace you
Who will listen?

En route

I have seen them when there was nothing else.
—W.S. Merwin

A catalpa leaf curving from moon,
a little broken in its passing.

A signal from the dead
drawn to me
like waves in love with the shore.

Ghost parents
patient as saxifrage that splits rocks
needing only to make amends.

Our first sunrise seen from earth,
their mother-father gaze,
our sea-coil of a song.

As I board the flight west
carrying cinnabons and sunglasses,
I wonder if they will follow me.

A wing, a roar, a leave-taking
over canopies of clouds —
grey white, grey rose, grey red.

Memories rust in my blue mind
like metal abandoned in rain.

Atoms rushing everywhere.
A brief perfect balance
between waking and dreams.

Once again muscle scrapes bone.
I see my parents waiting at the gate
wearing as many sleepless eyes
as they have feathers.

Ghost parents out-traveling me
to the lip of earth's surface world.

Derry in Time of Brexit

I drive through green fields, through the invisible
border fought over again in Brexit,
remembering the English woman's clipped syllables
echoing in the university office in Birmingham,
as everyday rain drummed the windows:
Why would anyone go to Ireland?
They have no history, do they?

Velvet hills hug the fraught city,
pubs filled and buzzing,
hotels unbombed for years now.
The political murals are predictable
but still make me cry
especially the one of the schoolgirl
who was shot by the British army.

And history's a ditch
for lying in, the Irish say, *if we let*
the gravediggers name us.

My father's father was an Ulsterman,
my mother's father from Limerick.
Walking a line — hard to do
in a cleaved world.

Orange, green, white,
the colors, weapons,
navy blue, deep red.
Tourists choose guides,
either Protestant or Catholic.
Or they take two walking tours,
two clashing cities here.

My father's father, Edward,
converted to marry Nellie from Galway.
He was a rock cleaved open.
Inside the rock, more rock.
An untouchable darkness.
We sat at the feet of his soundlessness.

Storefronts still boarded,
factories defunct, piles
of solid bricks for new construction,
bricks that once smashed windows.

My mother's father, Thomas,
died beneath a horse's hooves
when she was young.
Once horses were weapons of war.
Now they wander in waves of grass,
race on graceful ankles.

Hundreds of years…
One year…
History a river.

There is a peace bridge now,
built by the EU — ending in a park
where British soldiers once bunked.

But marchers still line up
to celebrate William of Orange,
their bright ribbons at odds
with drawn gaunt faces —
each one shut like a purse
around an old watch
that still keeps time.

There is a bell inside this memory

and a hand that rings it.
There's a playground of children
squeezed between red bricked school
and sandstone church,
lining up by our sizes
and I am always in the front
as we tumble and march
through the doors of classrooms
opening into wainscoted halls.

It's a kind of relief to come in —
jumpers, twirlers, shouters —

for those who played
and those like me who played at playing,
for those who watched, walking laps
at the edge of the schoolyard.
We all seemed to float away
like leaves turning in the wind.

It's good we are warming our desks again,
such cold little desks
screwed down to the floor.
How good and sleepy we feel
to know what we know…

The young nun will push her veil from her face.
The small hands on the clock will slowly circle,
and the thick brown shoes
we've kept tied all day
will take us home
through streets freshly tarred,

through scraggly empty lots
lilac bushes, bridal wreath and yards
where grass will not grow,
to our small crowded houses
fastened firmly to earth.

I remember my great grandfather in his corner,
lost in the smell of drifting pipe tobacco

and later the moon hiding from me behind trees,
the pattern of leaves on its face.

I come from the sound of the bell
and lace of broken moonlight.
Where else would I belong?

Fair

An old yellow streetcar.
So many chances before us.
Three steps and a window seat.
Waves of heat in the August air.

Chance was wide open.
The streetcar stopped at the gates.
Waves of heat rolled over us.
It was kids for free day at the fair.

We got off at Como and Snelling.
Coins in our pockets, a feast of booths before us.
We were full and forever and it was free this day.
Dreams were simple, a necklace strung bead by bead.

We walked the streets of the fair, our coins heavy.
Parents worried about polio, iron lungs, money, bombs.
Our dreams were beads fingered one by one.
The life we didn't know was the one we wanted.

Parents worried their fingers, polio and bombs.
What would we give now for the fair of innocence?
The life we didn't know was what we wanted.
Now what would we give for the smell of sweat in dust.

Three iron steps and a window seat.
The life we didn't know was the one we wanted.
What wouldn't we give to see the yellow streetcar
coming toward us through waves of August heat.

Carving the River Caves

Four thousand years make little difference
to teens skipping afternoon classes.

We find the smooth places in the rough sandstone,
old water marks, and carve there.
Sinews of calcite sculpt a leg, eyes are whorls
where the river fingered a fault-line.

Imagination's caverns cry out for symbols.
The glittering Mississippi unrolls
inexhaustible calligraphies.

We hunt lazy snakes on stones,
while barges tow the harvest south
and little fishing boats line up,

while our carved hearts and names shout
to the spiraling sun, the canoe moon.

Beads

Christ, crucifix, chalice —
by the time she's five she knows them.
Danger, she learns as the nuns drill her,
is a small lapse of attention.

Fierce women with closed, heavy faces
rule the school and the house.
Grandmother, mother,
their eyes, holes from too much seeing.

In the night she hears them.
Mother, Grandmother, herself —
all Marys. The nuns say, *Marry Jesus.*
Pray, they say, as if she could be pieced
into a quilt that will never be finished.

Her family prays rosaries in the car
on the way home from her grandmother's —
the joyful mysteries for driving down Selby,
all angels and announcements.

Then riding down West Seventh,
it's the sorrowful mysteries
filled with dead and dying.

Travail lives beside her,
familiar of her grandmother, mother.
The silence under their voices, blue.
But she wants an ecstasy of bells.

This is what they leave behind:
her grandmother's ruby ring,
    open-mouthed, like rain,
her mother's red rosary smoothed
by fingers praying through sicknesses,
    good byes, letting go.

Oak leaves stay on through winter
hissing and whispering,
    Everything moves.
    Even the dead.
    The earth is moving them for us.
    We can't teach you more than this.

She carries the glorious mysteries inside her —
    patterns in ice, in fire,
    earth spin and flight.

Crosby Dirt

The friendly young immigrant
who's helping me plant hydrangeas
wheels in a load of wet black dirt.

Got it at Crosby Park, he says.
River dirt bedding the plants,
Crosby already planted in my mind.

On Crosby rocks I kissed my high-school love,
embarrassed by a low flying plane
we thought was watching us.

Here, I exhausted my mother
walking her into the maze of green paths
with my young sons, farther than she dared.

From the green cathedral
    over my head, summer fruit is falling
        like the throb of a drum.

The Mississippi runs under the heat
        of the sun —
a throat choked with water,
a power drill at work on the river bridge piles.
Warnings prove its turbulence.

Hold your breath and you hear
    millennia of water
        sculpting limestone.

Past Crosby lake where our neighbor drowned
playing hockey, just below the hill
where Marty's sled flew into traffic.
We the so far lucky, the not-yet unlucky
litany their names.

In my yard, pink hydrangeas thrive
near a rock left by the last glacier.
At Crosby Park, the great river deepens its bed.

Over Bone Yards and Blossoms

For Mari and Libby, the two gymnasts

In the garden of the old house in St. Paul,
his fine mind saw a verdant island,
hawthorne and heart shaped blooms.

> *The mind of history is never still,*
> *its black thoughts, ravens...*

My great grandfather, nearing 100, planted roses
wearing a black vest, dangling watch chain.
At night he sang in two languages —
English, the clay;
Irish, the hand that shaped it.

His daughter, my Grandmother Mary, hated
the British. Memories of famine shadowed her,
whispering *there will never be enough.*
And there never was.
Widowed young with five children,
nothing in her hands.

Each month her cousin, John O'Connor,
stood at her door with money for her children.
He, the infamous Chief of Police
who took bribes from Al Capone in St. Paul.

> *The mind of history is never still,*
> *its white thoughts, ghost gulls*
> *tossing and cawing...*

My mother's mind was never still.
Her language, a stream through an overgrown garden,
a mix of Irish seeded English, old songs, histories,
roiling over ruins until the moment she died.

These days of arum lilies, acrobats and angels —
sometimes two young gymnasts flip down a blooming street.
I watch from my porch in the golden hours,
put down my glass of wine and loudly clap.

Coming Home

Tonight along the Mississippi, full moon on the river,
green lace-work softening the gap between branches.
I walk past the seminary, cross the small bridge.

Below, the ravine leads to the grotto
where I knelt in the dirt as a child
before a wide-armed Mary hewn from granite,
imagining I was Bernadette in the mud of Lourdes.

I remember how Jeanne and I,
two young nuns, crossed the river in spring
to visit my great uncle Jack in the ward for vets.
Rows of bedridden men without limbs
who cried because we stopped there.

These hopeful spring evenings one insistent crow
perching in an oak on the river bluff
summons others from their trees of learning
or their refuse heaps, calling them to roost.

In the same way, memories come home
as I return to the riverbank pulling the suitcase
of this body, this heart — their burden of light.

Equinox of my Brother's Death

For Jerry

Winters are hard. White tail deer
who survive feed in our yards
nosing around boulders, as if reading
Remember Me on the stones.

They nibble the ice fronds of willow.
We can see where the weight of their hooves
has made prints in the frozen ground,
small eruptions in our lives.

The deer are part of the story —
nature and our long history.
I miss your calls and tales
of need, escape, wildness.

And they said among themselves,
Who among us shall roll away the stone
from the door of the sepulcher?

You're here in the stories you told
the ones your brothers and I repeat —
of cars, of caves, of chaos rising
from your rivered world.

Your rebellions are still burning,
small fires on our road.
You know. You set them.

The Falling

The sky comes down behind the trees.
I walk through my old neighborhoods again.
Beneath branches of maple and oak,
a taste of rain — or snow.

I shuffle through leaf-fall, lift
my face to the almost intimate
light brushes of yellow-brown.

Down the line of trees into the curve
of land, I listen to the wind stop then stir,
nuzzling the branches.

The gentle hiss along the edge of drying grass,
a slant into light so still, so still —
I can hear the world happening.

Sometimes my old gods still visit here,
stand with me, whisper, then leave again
like those four great egrets rooted in the river mud
as if stillness were their one desire.

Red, Wolf, Eclipsing

Supermoon, Vernal Equinox, 2019

The last time the moon was this close
I waited beside Superior in cold light,
unbroken undulations of white, pock-marked
with shadows where waves had frozen in mid-thrash.

Moon says, *We are both full*
in our lucent veins, giving away our light.
But we are eclipsing, I say.
Everything touched by you
stays with you, she answers,
waits with you in the dark,
reappears incandescent.

The last time the super moon was so near
I set out to follow her, walking my heart
through frozen forests carrying the old,
wanting to be made new,
wanting to be blessed.

Tonight I watch the super moon
eclipse but I am not alone.
Grandma, is the moon a woman? Sylvie asks
Is that what they thought in history?
Is that what you think?
Yes, I answer, *yes to all of it.*

The last time the moon was blood,
wind, that all night howler, shook the windows.
Steam bears rose on wooly haunches
and marched over the bundled cloud-wall.

Red, Wolf, Eclipsing — hear
the grandmother in me howl.

IV

What's Left

Light, cross-stitch us
From stars and threads of moon,
Pour us forgiveness

Stone and Desire

At dusk when stone could crack open,
here comes that final fluted song —
all spiral and treble.
The leaf banked cardinal has unlocked
the sudden slim tunnel of its throat.

All evening the luna moths
cross thresholds of lily and hibiscus.
Bees nudge deep beyond orange clutches
of petals into widening honeysuckle emptiness.
Such forays like our own into the body,
deep notes of need.

We enter the liquid longing
of the cardinal's twilight song,
desire's shape sinuous
in the body's lonely splay.

In a Time of Distancing

For Conrad

Sometimes I just want to touch you
when I'm caught in the honeyed notes of the cello,
or hearing the chorus of gulls quarrel
at low-tide feast, the drumming of surf
in their throats.

I live in the silence between notes
between whistle-cries of the finches,
in the caesura of being present.

The world wants to be loved.
Andrea Bocelli sings for us
in hollow glitter of Milan Cathedral.

On the steps in front of soaring doors
and statues of the saved, he sings,
I was blind but now I see,

while videos of cities without people flash onscreen —
the Seine with no bookstalls,
Trafalgar with no traffic,
Times Square, a crazy tunnel echoing
the in-your-face circus that was.

The space between Tibetan bowl moon
and lavender sea buzzes with ions.
In the opera of what we're living through,
you help me stay grounded when stars call.
I touch you in the spaces of my longing.

Medieval Herbal

Let the man drink out of a church bell
yarrow   lupine   lichen   betony.
Let him sing while he drinks
Beati Immaculati.

Let the woman remain a virgin
until twenty-seven or eight.
Thus she will find her true origin.

Let her drink fennel against folly.

In her thirties when she is dry,
she should climb the Tor of St. Catherine,
pick purple monkshood, beware the poison
in the root, but taste true passion.

For heartache, give brambles —
pound the leaves, lay them over the breast
of both male and female.

At forty she will explode with pleasure.
Give her wild marjoram for a sore head,
the spirit plant parsley in good measure.

For the lunatic, give gentian and fennel.
Periwinkle brings grace; campion crowns victory.

The herb of greatest future is marigold.
Put it in the church where a woman sits
after breaking her matrimony.
It will not let her leave until desire is put away.

This has been proven true.

At fifty the body will quiet,
but she is not ready to stop.
Rosemary cures impotence
for men and women both.

Blessed be carnations for they
shall be called the flowers of god.
Grow pansies, love's casualty.

At sixty she finds wild roses
the size of her face
a sign of endurance.
Bluebells beneath beech trees
remind her of his eyes.

At seventy spider webs brush
against her face after rain.
She notices the fuzziness
of late summer leaves.

Her own skin feels fuzzy.
The hairs catch water.
Living without rue, low growing,
rain and sun touch all of her.

Blue Distance

Let's walk on Clamshell beach
the way we did so many summers.
Let's sit on the dock, feet in water
watching white birches tremble
in the glassy lake.

Here, my younger self calls to my life now.
Here is the young wife and mother I was.
Listen — the voices of children
who once were our own.

In the still waters of the bay,
reflections of birches
soften as lamplight is softened
in water's live shiver.

This is the place where our marriage
ended and began again.
Remember how lost we were.
Now anger spins itself out
in the gyre of past.

No time for future to repeat
the way every acorn and leaf
of the oak trees repeat.

Look, how great blue heron,
on a dead oak limb,
stares into the lake's
weed-dark mirror.

What we see when we gaze
long enough into the blue —
years flowing through us, my love,
making more of us than we can know.

Our Story

I was from down the hill, West Seventh's
huddled houses under Highland Park's
frowning doors and windows.

You were up the hill, that neighborhood of
churches like forts, tree-lined playgrounds.

Around Highland pool you charged, pushing us
girls screaming into the deep end. Your blond hair
bleached by sun. My pale skin reddening like my
Irish grandmas, black hair dripping.

Somehow I knew even then — so our story goes —
that fate would circle us round, when we were grown.

•••

Later, newly sprung from the convent, I had just
stumbled out of that bleak house
in Nordeast, free in butterfly yellow, no more
under the unblinking stare of my Superior.

One night in Dinkytown I asked a friend if he knew
a man with a beautiful soul and he called you,
fresh out of the Christian Brothers.

Remember how we drove together
to the Brothers' house on Summit to pick up
the papers releasing you from vows?
Your Superior predicted you'd end up
washing dishes somewhere.

We were a run-on sentence, escaping religion,
a winter that would not end, a road
with a single direction.

With a comma moon above us,
we merged like two worlds, two words.

Fifty years later, it's just you and me
through long, sun baked summers
and years washing dishes together,
slowing the night's long phrases
with our full stop bodies.

Medieval Consolations

To drink like Capuchins means drinking poorly.

To drink like Benedictines means drinking deeply.

Dominicans imbibe pot after pot.

We know Franciscans swill the cellars dry. *

God knows how Jesuits drink, says Britt, glass full.
You don't see me quaff, says Tim, glass empty.

I tell you this story:
When I was young a nun we stole red wine
from the altar in the dark of night,
took it to our tiny rooms, to sip.
On narrow beds we toasted, laughing hard.
My first, worst wine and best remembered

until that bottle emptied when we met,
for fifty years kept dust free on my shelf.

* *Heard on a London Pub Walk*

From the Fires

We thought at first it was the canopy
of a boat, but it kept rising from black water.

Not yet full it looked like a Monet
haystack burning orange with a red cast

color of dried blood. So deep it laid no path
across Lake Superior. No jewel maker this,

no ear drum, more glowing fossil
from a past we face, the future behind us.

We back into it, keep eyes on that orange kite,
caused they say by smoke blurring our sight.

Western forests burning — the old growth, the new.
Is there a fire in everything, a shining fossil fuel

beneath as saints believed? That moon a coal
sizzling in the prophet's mouth, you and I

on the lake walk, moored by words, by time,
watch a burning barge move toward us.

Water Lilies

Salle 1, L'Orangerie, Paris — quotes from Claude Monet

What I seek: Instantaneity

Like Orpheus, we are seduced
incandescent water gardens,
deep light at pond's edge
we hesitate, afraid to follow.

… especially the envelope

Blossoms swim into blue
Chartres, Della Robia, Fra Angelico
into green of seaweed — a rooted
writhing inside the wave.

the same light spreading everywhere…

Visitors whisper, swimming
in the light of paint —
melting candles of the lilies,
hours washed by art,
scoured by our years.

It's terrible how the light runs out.

Sunset tries to bargain with senescence.
We know stained glass starlight,
that dark light of the soul.

*A single lifetime is not long enough
to know even a single moment.*

Red Fox Running

For Conrad

First thing he sees near dawn
in the empty street is the fox,
almost hidden in autumn haze,
in yellow knotweed,
in crosshatched stalks, her lit fur.

Her gaze captures his;
her ears prick forward.
She is the color of oak leaves in fall,
copper and ginger streaked
with Lake Superior slate.

Hungry and another storm coming,
nose touches twig, leaf.
She bares her teeth, gnaws a sumac branch,
leaves paw prints in dew wet grass
before breaking from cover and running
toward a pond behind the houses.

She ignites the day for him.
Demands his attention,
burning through layers,
through holes in the air.

He runs, face browning, hair greying.
Later, as sweat rises from his nude body,
he sings into the silence, into unknown
neighborhoods of paws and pelts.

Ten Preludes in Blue

after hearing String Quartet No 1 "Ten Preludes" by Abrahamsen

Concealed in stillness
a doe nurses her spotted fawn,
taking pleasure in the warmth,
hunger moon forgotten.

•••

Our granddaughters dive from boat to lake —
the necklaced loon swims in to warn us away
from his brown fuzzed babies.

•••

High desert poppies flame.
White cones ignite on Joshua trees
tipped with thorns. Rattlesnakes
wind through mesquite below
the blue San Gabriel mountains —
hyacinths shivering with snow.

•••

With France's blooming trees
still trembling in our minds,
we sit on a bench watching waves.
Thumb-sized sandpipers whir
a rushing cloud over tide bed.
How do we speak about
the road we now must travel?

•••

Your eyes Pacific blue —
sun and sea and shore.
Let's go walking there.

•••

Low beds pocked with indigo —
eyes of the tide pools — white gulls,
white stones, facing into the wind.

•••

Their long bills clacking, red eyed
egrets shift from one foot to the other.
Watery dreams roll through us.

•••

Holy sundown, burning blue
of lapis, purple sea, islands
to the west, mountains east.
Fireball of sun suspended
between the arch of two palms.

•••

The concrete boardwalk
holds onto September heat.
We sit alone, the sweetness of wine
still on our lips and fingers.

•••

We will sleep back to back
beneath the waning moon.

Starlight on Waves

A fluting of finches in palm trees,
redwings or violin strings
older than language.
The storm idles over the mountain
revealing, dissolving
like bird song and string song.
That is why starlight,
called from hiding in cobalt and feathers,
plays the waves like notes
or the words of a child's book —
one word emerging from the page
to unroll its music suddenly everywhere.

•••

Listening to a Mendelssohn piano trio,
I am carried to a bridge,
leading to a world of unbreakable light.
I want to stay on the bridge and listen
to the way cello and violin
touch and separate.
The piano behind them
sometimes interrupts, sometimes protects.
A repetition of melody, the same and different —
urgent like the notes of starlight on waves,
green as the sliver of lime in a glass,
ice light and lamp light.

•••

My hungry heart always wants to stay,
wants another twelve years with you
to add to our fifty, even though the sea
has played all its notes of blue and lavender.
I want one more book to read,
one more day to write
the way a child writes, above the lines,
as if all words weren't written on water.
I want to live on the bridge that music makes
listening to some enormity, elsewhere but not far.
Bridge that crosses, and scatters the dark.

The Colors of Pain

The Church at Auvers (Vincent Van Gogh, 1890)

For forty years, I've studied the print
on my bedroom wall — how the painter's
swift strokes make the stone church
launch itself, violet-hued
from millefleured earth into pure cobalt.

A shattered knee brought me
to this before and after moment —
paint strokes related to my life.

Today I see how Vincent's yellow blooms
along the sandy road are licked with light
while the church explodes, rises
and rests in its dark blue agony.

Window spaces streak ultramarine.
Purple and orange patch the roof.
Bell tower leans, dark and empty.

Vincent's paths diverged toward pain.
This sand-colored, shadowed walk, splits
and snakes around the church at Auvers
as a bent woman walks past it.

Vincent shows me the way light changes
everything in the life of a single day.
Riverine indigo and lemon yellow
shaped me, made me what I am.

For All That is Lost

It's easy to love forgotten fields,
pathless woods, empty lots.

I will be a scavenger of life
in a new wilderness.

I embrace the misplaced beauty
of overgrown ditches —
nettles, thistles, blackthorn.

Praise no man's land —
plastic bags, broken bottles,
gulls feeding on garbage,

fish near sewage pipes, bear
lurking near the dump, pathogens
freed to kill us

while on the edges, ravens
try over and over
their broken notes.

Blueing

The blue eye charms in every Turkish market,
to ward off evil, the same periwinkle on doors
in every hill village in Portugal
blue squeezed from leaves
of the yellow flowering woad plant.

The same woad blue the Picts used
to paint their bodies
like the blue nude by Matisse
and the bodies of Cezanne's bathers —
blue blotched the way the sky
is cloud blotched.

•••

Lapis lazuli, original blue mined from earth
in Afghanistan, ground to aquamarine of illuminations,
found in the teeth of a medieval female
scribe, ground to paint the Virgin's gown
in centuries of Annunciations.

Fra Angelico's blue of Mary's gown, sky flowing.
The angel all tenderness — longing rains
over his ambiguous face. Her whole body
a question — all tilt, eyes frightened,
forgotten book dropped in the lap.

Once, a blue fog rose on the lake
revealing a fishing boat. I heard the whine
of its motor before I saw my children
wave their small arms —
turning wings loved by azure wind
bringing them home to me.

•••

Earth gave us blue.
Cobalt above and within all things.

In my mind, the hands and arms
that hold me wear the pregnant
blue of the sea before sunset.
For a moment, sky and earth
the same aquamarine.

We are blue smoke, mineral, ether
temporary against eternal hills.
Blue-veined sky breathes birds
in and out of the light,
their breasts glowing sapphires.

•••

At closing time, when the guard comes
into the empty Prado, I'm still leaning
into that impossible blue of the Virgin,
into that deepening sky.

The Spinning Universe: Konya, Turkey

I

The Dance

Love waited in every doorway for Rumi.

It sent him whirling,
>   *I am so small I can barely be seen.*
>   *How can this great love be inside me?*

a dance he taught his teacher,
Shams of Tabriz,
and all the dervishes.
>   *Look at your eyes. They are small,*
>   *But they see enormous things.*

The dance doesn't speak
in any known tongue.
Rumi taught Shams to spin, to let stars
take over the field of his mind.

This day dervishes whirl
outside the dark room where Rumi
dreamed the ecstatic dance.

Tulip shaped saffron colored gowns
shade the light of their bodies.
I don't know if they belong to the earth
or to the air.

With them I rise toward the clouds,
deep blue, flowing into the future.
With them I see how prayer might live in us
if we would let it.
How time circles in us.
What it means to be ecstatic in love.

II

The Women

Through a market place

of burka clad women,
my friend and I follow
a golden spire
to the poet's emerald tiled tomb
where more women
chant and bow.

We bend to enter the dark cell where he
slept on a cot, prayed and wrote —
Qur'an, parchment with stylus —
his sandals upon the 800 year old floor.

My Turkish friend despairs:

Ten years ago women in this city
were all dressed like you and me.
Now look at them — pressured to be covered.
In black we are going backward.
I have a plan to get my daughter out, if I need to.

III

The Prayer

Rumi, teach us to see
our path of light, of love
while history and governments
whirl away like planetary dust.

Illuminations

While feathers went on falling in the doorways
　　　　　　　　　　　　　　　　—W.S. Merwin

1

In a dream the Buddha gives me
three white stones,
tells me —

Keep these on your table
　　to remind you of what they are

simply stones
　　nothing to be afraid of

When you see them scattered on the trail
　　common as clover

bow to them
　　your sisters

2

I wake up knowing my scarlet flower
heart has sheltered too long
underground.

I have forgotten more times
than gulls follow the flight path
how to be easy
when the world turns red.

Unburied heart,
open now
to the meadow-ripe bird-world

lava field with shasta daisies
grey beach stones suddenly erupting
into white wild phlox.

Above the ever-blooming surf
a braid of young pelicans unspools,
slim and surprising in their grace
flanked by egrets — their wings on fire.

White stones illumine my table —
yesterday, today and tomorrow.

Give way, unsheltered heart.
Give away your light.

Notes

Thank you to California poet, Maia whose work has nourished mine for many years. I acknowledge this debt of creative inspiration. The following poems in particular are indebted to her work: *Vanishing* (especially the last stanza), *Music for a Sleepless Night* (after Sleepless Nights), *Alphabets, In a Time of Distancing*.

Stone and Desire owes a debt to work by Jude Nutter.

Derry in a time of Brexit owes a debt to work of Maureen McClane; italicized lines are from This Blue.

Among the Kingdoms is after a poem by Stephen Linsteadt.

There is a bell and *Latigo Canyon* are inspired by the work of Kathy Fagan.

Italicized lines in *The Songs* are from **77 Dreams Songs** (# 66) by John Berryman.

The Songs is after a poem by Clare Rossini

The Falling is after a poem by Nina Bogen.

Italicized lines in *Over Boneyards and Blossoms* are from **Two Trips to Ireland** by David Young.

Still Life with Lemons, Oranges and a Rose by *Francisco de Zurbaran, 1633* is in the European collection at the (Norton Simon Museum) in Pasadena, CA.

Hallowed Ground is the title of an art book by painter and photographer Gaal Shepherd.

In the south central region of the vast Anatolian steppe in Turkey, the city of *Konya* is the site of the tomb and museum of Rumi, the thirteenth century Persian poet.

About the Author

marykayrummel. com

Mary Kay Rummel was the first Poet Laureate of Ventura County, CA. *Nocturnes: Between Flesh and Stone* is her ninth published poetry book, her seventh full collection. Blue Light Press also published *Cypher Garden, The Lifeline Trembles* (a winner of the 2014 Blue Light Press Award) and *What's Left is the Singing. This Body She's Entered*, her first book, won the Minnesota Voices Award for poetry and was published by New Rivers Press in 1989. It was a finalist for the Minnesota Book Award. Her work has appeared in numerous regional, national and international literary journals and anthologies and has received several awards, including a Loft Mentor Award and eight Pushcart nominations. She was a co-editor of *Psalms of Cinder & Silt*, a collection of community poems related to recent California wildfires published by Glenna Luschei at Solo Press.

Mary Kay has read her poems in many venues in the US, England and Ireland and has been a featured reader at poetry festivals including in Ojai and San Luis Obisbo, CA. She has participated in numerous poetry residencies and workshops and loves to perform poetry with musicians. Born in St. Paul, she has been on the faculties of the University of Minnesota, Minneapolis and Duluth campuses and California State University, Channel Islands. She is a board member of the nonprofit Ventura County Poetry Project. She and her husband, Conrad, live in California and Minnesota, near children and grandchildren in both states.

Poetry Books by Mary Kay Rummel

Cypher Garden, Blue Light Press, 2017

The Lifeline Trembles, Blue Light Press, 2014, winner of Blue Light Award

What's Left Is The Singing, Blue Light Press, 2010

Love in the End: A chapbook, Bright Hill Press, 2008

The Illuminations, Cherry Grove, 2006

Green Journey, Red Bird, Loonfeather Press, 2000

The Long Journey Into North: A chapbook, Juniper Press 1999

This Body She's Entered, A Minnesota Voices Award Winner at New Rivers Press, 1989, finalist for the Minnesota Book Award

Nonfiction Books (written with Elizabeth Quintero)

Storying: A Path to the Future, Peter Lang International

Becoming a Teacher: Connecting classrooms and communities, Peter Lang

Teachers' Reading/Teachers' Lives, SUNY Press

American Voices: Webs of Diversity, Merrill/McMillan Publishing

About the Cover Artist

Charles Karp is a southern California oil painter with a studio in Camarillo, California. His art work includes landscape, portrait and still life paintings.

He says about his work:

Although I drew enthusiastically as a teenager, I received no formal art training. After pursuing other careers, I moved to southern California and began painting in 2007. I sought out accomplished painters in the area who were teaching in a traditional atelier style. Among them were Ignat Ignatov, Michael Siegel, David Gallup, Jeremy Lipking, Sean Cheetham, Noble Powell, Tony Pro, Ron Lemen, and Johanna Spinks.

My painting "November Sunset off Malibu" was painted alla prima during a late November afternoon from atop a cliff overlooking the Pacific Ocean.

In addition to numerous juried exhibitions, a number of my portrait, landscape and still life paintings have been sold to private collections in California, Hawaii, Oregon and internationally in Florence and Rome, Italy.

Most recently I was selected as a Visiting Artist at the American Academy in Rome in 2019 and again in 2020. While in residence at the Academy I painted a series of portrait studies inspired by sculptures of ancient Roman and Etruscan figures whose faces I found particularly expressive. In addition I was honored to paint portraits of Liana Brent and Victoria Moses, two Rome Prize winners in Ancient Studies, for the Academy's archival gallery of Rome Prize recipients.

My artist web site is www.charleskarp.com.